# WHAT'S IN YOUR HAMBURGER?

Jaclyn Sullivan

**PowerKiDS** press.

New York

*To Mom and Dad, even though I never liked your hamburgers*

Published in 2012 by The Rosen Publishing Group, Inc,
29 East 21st Street, New York, NY 10010

First Edition

Editor: Sara Antill
Book Design: Greg Tucker

Photo Credits: Cover, pp. 4, 7, 9 (top, bottom), 10, 12, 13 (top, bottom), 15 (bottom), 17, 19, 20–21, 21 (right) Shutterstock.com; p. 5 BananaStock/Thinkstock; p. 6 Art Shay/Time & Life Pictures/Getty Images; p. 8 Noel Hendrickson/Digital Vision/Thinkstock; p. 11 © www.iStockphoto.com/Muammer Mujdat Uzel; p. 14 © www.iStockphoto.com/Juanmonino; p. 15 (top) Xavier Testelin/Gamma-Rapho via Getty Images; p. 16 Photodisc/Thinkstock; p. 20 (left) Jack Hollingsworth/Photodisc/Thinkstock; p. 22 Image Source/Getty Images.

Library of Congress Cataloging-in-Publication Data

Sullivan, Jaclyn.
 What's in your hamburger? / by Jaclyn Sullivan. — 1st ed.
    p. cm. — (What's in your fast food)
 ISBN 978-1-4488-6211-5 (library binding) — ISBN 978-1-4488-6381-5 (pbk.) —
ISBN 978-1-4488-6382-2 (6-pack)
 1. Hamburgers—Juvenile literature. 2. Convenience foods—Juvenile literature. I. Title.
 TX370.S85 2012
 641.6'6—dc23
                                    2011032106

Manufactured in the United States of America

CPSIA Compliance Information: Batch #WW12PK: For Further Information contact Rosen Publishing, New York, New York at 1-800-237-9932

# Contents

# Hello, Hamburger!

Our bodies get energy from food. We need energy for everything we do. This boy is using energy to ride a skateboard.

If you walk into any fast-food restaurant in the United States, you will probably see hamburgers on the menu. Hamburgers are also popular at parties and barbecues. Have you ever wondered what a hamburger is made of? Knowing what is in the foods we eat is very important.

Different foods give our bodies different **nutrients**. Our bodies need nutrients to keep our muscles

Many people enjoy eating hamburgers at picnics and other outdoor events. Hamburgers can be cooked on outdoor grills, and you do not need knives, forks, or plates to eat them!

growing, our blood flowing, and our brains working. Your body works best when you give it healthy foods that have the nutrients it needs. This book will help you find out if hamburgers are a good choice for your body.

Ray Kroc, seen here, bought the McDonald's restaurant chain from the McDonald brothers in 1961. He helped McDonald's grow into a very successful business with restaurants all over the world.

Over the years, many people have claimed that they invented the hamburger. Some people think that the hamburger was actually invented by a teenager! In 1885, a 15-year-old boy named Charlie Nagreen was selling meatballs at a fair in Wisconsin. He smashed some of the meatballs between two slices of bread so people could walk around the fair and eat at the same time. Soon other people started making these hamburger sandwiches.

Hamburgers were named after the city of Hamburg, Germany, seen here. The meat used in early hamburgers reminded people of a German dish called Hamburg steak.

Then, in 1948, Richard and Maurice McDonald opened the first McDonald's restaurant. Hamburgers were the main item on the McDonald's menu. McDonald's restaurants started opening all over the United States. As McDonald's got more famous, so did the hamburger!

# Beef Patties

The flat, round meat of a hamburger is called the **patty**. It is made of ground beef, which comes from cows. The beef used to make fast-food hamburgers can come from many parts of a cow. The most common place for the beef to come from is near the shoulder of the cow. This cut of beef is called chuck.

Some ground beef has more fat in it than other kinds. If you are not sure what the numbers on a package of meat mean, ask your parents or someone who works in the grocery store.

Chuck has more fat in it than some other cuts of beef. The next time you are in a grocery store, look at the different packages of ground beef. You might see a number such as 80/20. That would mean that 20 percent of the meat is made of fat.

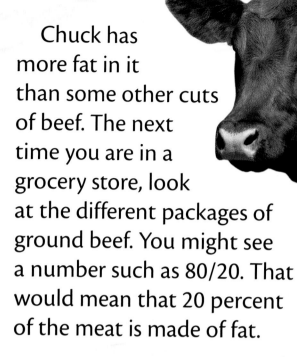

Beef comes from cows. Although the word "hamburger" might lead you to believe they do, hamburgers do not have any ham in them at all!

## FAST-FOOD FACTS

Did you know that ground beef has not actually been ground up? The beef is finely chopped in a machine. It can then be formed into the flat, round shape of a hamburger patty.

# Hamburger Buns

To make a hamburger, the cooked patty is placed on a bun. Hamburger buns are made in bread factories. The main **ingredient** in a hamburger bun is flour, which comes from a type of grass called wheat. The flour is mixed with water, sugar, and a living thing called yeast. The yeast makes the bread dough rise. The dough is then rolled into ball shapes and baked.

Most fast-food and packaged hamburger buns

Wheat is grown in large fields. People use machines called combine harvesters, like the one seen here, to gather wheat. The wheat can then be turned into flour.

These hamburger buns are about to be put into a large oven and baked. Then, they will be packaged and sent to grocery stores and restaurants.

need to stay fresh longer than they naturally would. For this reason, **preservatives** are often added to the dough. Preservatives keep the buns soft while they are shipped to fast-food restaurants and grocery stores.

# All the Fixings

When cheese is added to a hamburger, it is called a cheeseburger. Like beef, cheese comes from cows. Cheese is made from the milk of a cow.

Some people like to use **condiments**, like ketchup and mustard, on their hamburgers. Pickles are a popular topping on most fast-food hamburgers. Lettuce, tomatoes, and onions often come on hamburgers, too. Adding lettuce and tomatoes to

Tomatoes grow on vines. Tomatoes are green at first. They turn red as they get ripe, or ready to eat.

your hamburger is an easy way to add **vitamins** and nutrients to your meal. Tomatoes have a lot of vitamin C in them. Vitamin C helps your body fight off illnesses. Lettuce has vitamin K, which keeps your blood healthy.

This boy is eating a hamburger topped with ketchup and cheese. Cheese has calcium, which helps your bones stay strong.

## FAST-FOOD FACTS

Pickles are actually cucumbers that have been soaked in vinegar or very salty water called brine. The word "pickle" comes from the Dutch word *pekel,* which means "brine."

# The Other Stuff in Hamburgers

To make a hamburger patty at home, you would probably use ground beef and perhaps some onions and salt for taste. The hamburgers at fast-food restaurants have other things added to them, though. Like the buns, most fast-food hamburgers have preservatives. The preservatives keep things that can make us sick from growing on the beef.

When foods are **processed**, they lose a lot of their color and flavor. The beef used to make fast-food hamburgers is a

The next time you get a hamburger from a fast-food restaurant, try smelling it. The strong scents you smell likely come from spices and chemicals added to the beef patty, not the beef itself.

processed food. Fast-food restaurants often add **artificial** colors and dyes to make the beef look browner than it really is. Artificial flavors add back the beef flavor that was lost in processing.

Here, lettuce and pickles are being placed on hamburger buns at a fast-food restaurant. The vinegar or brine that pickles are soaked in acts as a natural preservative.

## FAST-FOOD FACTS

Ketchup is a sauce made from tomatoes, vinegar, sugar, and other ingredients. You might think a tomato is a vegetable. It is actually a fruit, though!

# Protein and Fat

When a hamburger patty is cooked, some of the fat in it melts away.

Most people would not think of a hamburger as a healthy food. However, eating hamburgers once in a while does not have to be bad for you. The ground beef used to make the hamburger patty has a lot of **protein**. Protein is a nutrient that our bodies need to keep our muscles strong.

Ground beef can also have a lot of fat, though. Our bodies need some fat to stay healthy. However, too much fat can make you sick. Extra

Our bodies need protein. Protein helps build muscles and also helps muscles heal if they are stretched or torn.

fat can cause waxy stuff called **cholesterol** to build up in your body. Too much cholesterol makes it hard for your heart to pump blood.

## Nutrition Facts

Serving Size 4 oz. (237g)
Servings Per Container: 1

**Amount Per Serving**

**Calories** 531     Calories from Fat 192

**% Daily Value \***

| | |
|---|---|
| **Total Fat** 21g | 35% |
| Saturated Fat 7g | 35% |
| Trans Fat 0g | |
| **Cholesterol** 68mg | 25% |
| **Sodium** 711mg | 30% |
| **Total Carbohydrate** 54g | 20% |
| Dietary Fiber 3g | 10% |
| Sugar 3g | |
| **Protein** 29g | 58% |

| | | |
|---|---|---|
| Vitamin A 0% | • | Vitamin C 8% |
| Calcium 15% | • | Iron 30% |

*Percent Daily Values are based on a 2,000 calorie diet. Your daily values may be higher or lower depending on your calorie needs.

| | Calories | 2,000 | 2,500 |
|---|---|---|---|
| Total Fat | Less than | 65g | 80g |
| Sat Fat | Less than | 20g | 25g |
| Cholesterol | Less than | 300mg | 300mg |
| Sodium | Less than | 300mg | 300mg |
| Total Carbohydrate | | 300g | 375g |
| Dietary Fiber | | 25g | 30g |

Calories per gram:

Fat 9    •    Carbohydrate 4    •    Protein 4

You can learn more about what is in your hamburger by reading the label. The label might be on the hamburger wrapper or on the restaurant Web site. The label will tell you how much of each nutrient and vitamin is in your food. Fiber, fat, and protein are all nutrients. The bigger the number is next to each nutrient, the more of it there is in your hamburger.

This is an example of a label on a fast-food hamburger. You can see here that one serving, or one hamburger, gives you 30 percent of the sodium you should have in one day to stay healthy.

Kids need between 1,600 and 1,800 calories every day to stay healthy. Fast-food meals can add a lot of calories to your diet.

The number of **calories** in a hamburger is also listed on the label. Calories measure how much energy is in our food. We need the energy from food to survive. Eating more calories than we need can make us gain weight, though.

# Healthier Hamburgers

There are ways to make a healthier hamburger. Lean beef has less fat than regular beef. If you use lean beef to make a hamburger, you will get more healthy protein and less unhealthy fat. You can also use whole-wheat hamburger buns. Whole-wheat buns are made with whole-wheat flour and have a lot of fiber. Fiber helps you **digest** your food.

This family is shopping for lettuce at the grocery store. Types of lettuce with darker green leaves often have more nutrients than lettuce with lighter green leaves.

Fresh vegetable toppings are also healthy and delicious on hamburgers. Lettuce, tomato, and onion are very popular. Other toppings, like pineapple and mushrooms, can be used, too. Try different things to see what you like best!

*Top*: This girl is growing tomatoes in a backyard garden. You can add other things from a garden, such as peppers, to your hamburger, too.
*Left*: Many people enjoy adding a slice of pineapple to their hamburgers. You can even try using pineapple to replace the hamburger patty!

# Choose Wisely

A hamburger can be a filling lunch during the school day. This boy has added an apple and a carton of milk to his lunch.

You can make good choices about the food you eat. Hamburgers can be part of a healthy **diet**. Talk to your parents about making hamburgers at home instead of eating fast-food hamburgers. If you do eat a fast-food hamburger or if you have a hamburger for lunch at school, ask for healthy toppings like lettuce and tomatoes.

When you make healthy choices, you are taking good care of your body. When you take care of your body, you feel your best!

# Glossary

**artificial** (ar-tih-FIH-shul) Made by people, not nature.

**calories** (KA-luh-reez) Amounts of food that the body uses to keep working.

**cholesterol** (kuh-LES-teh-rohl) A fatty material that can build up in one's body and increase one's chance of getting heart disease.

**condiments** (KON-duh-ments) Seasonings or sauces added to a food to give it flavor.

**diet** (DY-ut) Food that people and animals normally eat.

**digest** (dy-JEST) To break down food so that the body can use it.

**ingredient** (in-GREE-dee-unt) Something that goes into food.

**nutrients** (NOO-tree-ents) Food that a living thing needs to live and grow.

**patty** (PA-tee) A small, flat mass of ground or chopped food.

**preservatives** (prih-ZER-vuh-tivz) Substances that keep something from going bad.

**processed** (PRAH-sesd) Something that is treated or changed using a special series of steps.

**protein** (PROH-teen) An important element inside the cells of plants and animals.

**vitamins** (VY-tuh-minz) Nutrients that help the body fight illness and grow strong.

# Index

**B**
beef, 8–9, 12, 14–16, 20
bodies, 4–5, 13, 16–17, 22
bun(s), 10–11, 14, 20

**C**
cheese, 12
color(s), 14–15
condiments, 12
cow(s), 8, 12

**D**
diet, 22

**F**
fat, 9, 16–18, 20
fiber, 18, 20
flour, 10, 20

**I**
ingredient, 10

**L**
lettuce, 12–13, 21–22

**M**
meat, 8–9
meatballs, 6
menu, 4, 7
muscles, 4, 16

**N**
Nagreen, Charlie, 6
nutrient(s), 4–5, 13, 16, 18

**O**
onion(s), 12, 14, 21

**P**
patty, 8, 10, 14, 16
people, 6, 12, 16
pickles, 12
preservatives, 11, 14

**R**
restaurant(s), 4, 7, 11, 14–15

**T**
teenager, 6
tomato(es), 12–13, 21–22

**V**
vitamin(s), 13, 18

**W**
wheat, 10

# Web Sites

Due to the changing nature of Internet links, PowerKids Press has developed an online list of Web sites related to the subject of this book. This site is updated regularly. Please use this link to access the list:

www.powerkidslinks.com/food/burger/